ERYRI
The Story of Snowdonia

First published in 1999
New colour edition: 2011

© Text: Michael Senior

ISBN: 978–1-84524-165-0

Cover design: Eirian Evans

Published by Gwasg Carreg Gwalch,
12 Iard yr Orsaf, Llanrwst, Wales LL26 0EH
tel: 01492 624031
fax: 01492 641502
email: books@carreg-gwalch.com
internet: www.carreg-gwalch.com

ERYRI

The Story of Snowdonia

Michael Senior

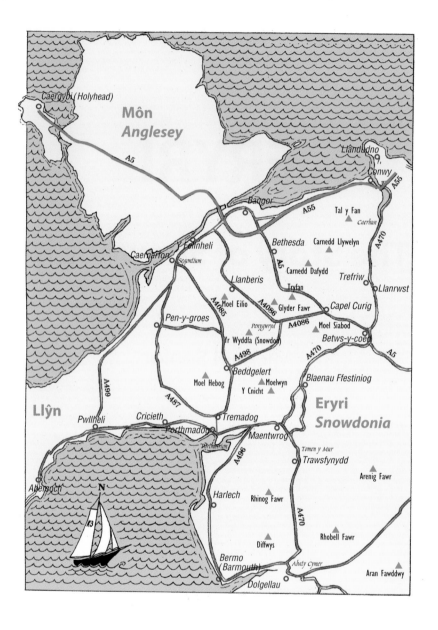

Contents

Note to the new edition
This edition includes material previously published in
The Conwy Valley and its long history and *Meirionnydd's Story.*

Snowdonia through the seasons – May on the shores of Llyn Gwynant, with a view of the Aran ...

... and winter snow at Nant y Benglog

Introduction

> I must not pass over in silence the mountains called by the Welsh Eryri, but by the English Snowdon, or Mountains of Snow, which gradually increasing from the land of the sons of Conan, and extending themselves northwards near Deganwy, seem to rear their lofty summits even to the clouds, when viewed from the opposite coast of Anglesey.

So Giraldus noted, on his journey through Wales in 1188. This proves the ancientness of both terms, but while it explains probably quite correctly the origins of the name 'Snowdon' (the 'don' part coming from the same Saxon word which gave us 'dune' and 'down'), it does not offer help with 'Eryri'. It was George Borrow who established the modern conventional wisdom: it was called Eryri 'by the Britons, because in the old time it abounded with eagles, Eryri in the ancient British language signifying an eyrie or breeding-place of eagles.' There is no doubt that the Welsh word for eagle is 'eryr'. Borrow hints in a footnote at something which has been more firmly established by Sir Ifor Williams, that there was a root word 'er' meaning 'to rise' from which both these words come: the rising place, and the rising bird. 'It is possible,' runs Borrow's footnote, 'that many will be disposed to maintain that in the case of Snowdon the word is intended to express a rugged excrescence or eruption on the surface of the earth.'

Pennant (who coined the name Snowdonia) disagrees. He thinks that the Welsh term means the same as the English, and that Creigiau'r Eryri, the Eagle Rocks, is simply a mistransliteration of 'Creigiau'r Eira', the snowy crags. His editor then confuses the whole thing further by saying that this seems to be a translation of Snowdon back into Welsh which was anyway a mistranslation in the first place, of Eryri, the eagle country, as 'eiry', snowy.

To Borrow Snowdon was 'no single hill' but a region. He does not use Pennant's term. Now the first name is normally used to refer to a single group of peaks, the second to the region as a whole, as in the Snowdonia National Park. This is the same region covered by the term, whatever its origins (though I personally am with Sir Ifor Williams), Eryri.

It is the upland zone. It is defined by contrast. Two valleys limit two of its flanks, to east and south in almost rectangular lines. It falls sharply to a coastal plain, and at one point to the sea itself, in the north; and in the west the Dwyfor valley separates it sharply from the Llŷn peninsula.

Clogwyn Du'r Arddu

Cwm Idwal

The Making of the Mountains

The geology of Snowdonia is immensely complex, one result of which is that any attempt to do it full justice immediately becomes tedious. There are so many qualifications which must be made and sub-divisions inserted. The great geologists who have written about this area, such as Greenly and North, struggle with the dilemma of trying to convey accurate information while telling an almost incredible tale. On the face of it, it is hard to make something so apocalyptic sound dull; yet science can find a way.

Here I want to sketch a kind of synopsis, which will, however, remain true to the underlying complexity, and which will, I hope, convey the salient points of the aeon-long saga.

What we see in Eryri is the residue of a largely destroyed landmass which was itself originally the reworked debris of an anciently vanished land. What we regard as high peaks today are the worn-away remnants of a much vaster smooth-sided shallow sloped dome. If this seems improbable enough it is outdone by the next point. The whole of this was laid down in the form of even layers of sediment under an anciently vanished sea.

So long ago that it would be futile to rehearse the millions there was another country here. In the course of enough time, and in conditions where rainfall is possible, everything in the end gets worn away. The pressure of one layer on another, and the sea above them, gradually formed the sediments into bands of rock. Two things then occurred to complicate the issue, both of them consisting of forms of pressure caused by the nature of the earth's core and crust. Molten matter forced its way through weaknesses in the strata, some of it remaining embedded in them, some bursting through to fall back onto the sea's floor. All this so far gave rise to horizontal even layers. It was another sort of pressure, this time coming from each side, which caused the layers to become buckled or folded, forcing the upper parts of the resulting undulation up out of the sea, where, incidentally, they could become eroded again by rain and return as sediment to take their part again in the age-long cycle.

In rough schematic form it goes like this. 1. Deposition. 2. Uplift. 3. Erosion. The erosion gives rise to deposition again and the whole thing starts again, repeated a presumably infinite number of times.

We see Eryri today in the middle of one of its phases of erosion. If we had

Clogwyn y Garnedd, and Snowdon summit above Llyn Glaslyn

been here some hundred million years ago we would have seen a vast high gently rising plateau. If we could wait long enough we would observe it all levelled off again, slipping finally into an all-embracing sea. Except that it would not of course be 'final'. In due course another Snowdonia would be thrust up and go through this whole process again.

In the meantime, since this is the time we happen to be here, let us take a closer look at the Eryri which we have, and consider exactly how it came to be the way it is. As far as the matter it is made of is concerned, there are some simple distinctions which may be made.

The mountains are made of two broad groups of rocks, the sedimentary rocks which are the deposits of the eroded older land, and the igneous rocks which have been blown out of the earth's core. The latter appear on the surface in two different ways, either having erupted there or having infiltrated the strata of sedimentary rock and been revealed by erosion. Rhyolite, the name of which comes from the Greek word 'to flow', is a common version of the first form, lava which has poured out and cooled fast. This forms the peaks of several of the higher mountains, characterised by their sharpness, such as Tryfan and Snowdon. The other type of igneous rock, which has

Tryfan

cooled far below ground and so more slowly, is of a coarser texture in which crystals have had time to form, and which often also contains seams of minerals for the same reason. Part of Crib Goch are of this form, and the bulk of Penmaenmawr and Foel Fras in the northern uplands.

The oldest rocks can be regarded as the base on which the mountains were built, and appear in our area mainly in a craggy ridge running south-west from near Bethesda across the bottom of Llyn Padarn. These are known as Pre-Cambrian, being older than the Cambrian series so named by Sedgwick, and are part of the original make-up of the earth. The enormous resistance of the Padarn ridge explains another feature of this immediate area, the incidence on either flank of the Elidirs of massive accumulations of slate.

Slate is squashed mud. It owes its fissile nature to the position of its particles relative to the line of pressure which compressed it, and also to the presence of thin layers of minerals within them. The great quarries of Bethesda and Llanberis owe their ultimate origins to the flow of lava and sediment from the Snowdon area pushing material ahead of it up against the immovable barrier of the Padarn ridge.

Nant Ffrancon

Glacier rocks and water erosion
in Nant Ffrancon

The geological periods which the rocks developed which made the mountains are divided into three, in which there are many component phases. If we consider that the last of these, known as the Tertiary Era, was the shortest of the three we get some inkling of the time-scale involved. It lasted more than sixty million years. Compared to that everything that has happened since can be regarded as recent and relatively fast.

Starting about a million years ago this part of the world began to get significantly colder. Climate changes occur largely as a result of solar activity, though it is sometimes speculated that unexpectedly sudden change could be brought about by an asteroid impact, the dust-cloud from which could filter out the sun. The effect, in any case, is that when the climate cools the winter ice fails to melt during the summer, and gradually increases in thickness.

The form of the land, when it became covered in ice, was basically as it is now; the ice modified its details. It was because the valleys already existed that the glaciers slid down them, borne by gravity downwards. As they slid they scoured away the jutting spurs and smoothed the valley bottoms. A river valley has a V-shaped profile, a glacial valley is shaped like a U. Nant Ffrancon is, famously, the perfect example of a glacial valley.

The area in general is widely littered with the signs of the ice's presence, its retreat and its eventual melting. So plain is this to us today that it is odd to think that until the 1840's it was not recognised that we had undergone an ice age at all F.J. North, in his section on geology in 'Snowdonia', quotes a note by Charles Darwin that is worth repeating. He and Adam Sedgwick had been in Cwm Idwal in 1831 looking for fossils. They examined all the rocks with extreme care, 'but neither of us saw a trace of the wonderful glacial phenomena all around us. We did not notice the plainly scored rocks, the perched boulders, the lateral and terminal moraines. Yet these phenomena are so conspicuous that a house burnt down by fire did not tell its story more plainly than did this valley. If it had still been filled by a glacier the phenomena would have been less clear than they now are'.

Darwin was in Cwm Idwal again in 1842, by which time no doubt his eyes were opened. Indeed Cwm Idwal has much to teach us about the ice ages, in particular the fact that there was more than one. It has in fact no less than four terminal moraines, representing the stages of withdrawal of the ice, between which they show that there was temporary renewal.

Llyn Llydaw

Nant Peris

Llanberis pass

14

A terminal moraine is the load of stones carried down by the glacier and deposited at its end, the point at which it stopped and then melted. We often see them, in fact, on our beaches. Up here in the hills they show us the extent of the late glaciers, as things began to warm up on the plains below. Their effect, by acting as a dam, is to give us mountain lakes. It is doubtful that without this, and the gouging out by the ice of rock basins, there would be any lakes in our area. The lakes are a glacial feature.

Lateral moraine is the burden of stones, fallen from the cliffs scraped and gnawed by the ice, which were deposited as it melted along its flanks. They can tell us the glaciers' thickness. We can also see their extent by the scratched and smoothed rocks which Darwin referred to, the side facing the oncoming ice being as if moulded, the side away from it often broken off and so sharp and jagged.

From these signs we can see that every valley had its glacier, the largest being in the Ogwen valley, where, in its upper stretches, it was over a thousand feet thick. A large glacier also filled the Llanberis valley, fed by two tributaries off Snowdon, from Cwm y Glas Mawr and Bach. Six glaciers ran off Snowdon altogether, two (from Cwm y Llan and Cwm Dyli) joining the Nant Gwynant glacier, and two going off on their own from Cwm Brwynog and Cwm Clogwyn.

The ice in the main valleys thus gained its mass and depth, and in the process its quarrying effect cut off the bottoms of the tributary glaciers to leave, now, 'hanging valleys'. When the ice fell back the last glaciers to linger caused the mountains to crumble back to the hardest rock of their makeup, leaving us with the cliffs at the back of Snowdonia's characteristic cwms, those small and deep lake-filled rock basins, carved by the last ice and dammed by its moraine, which usually face north-east, where the ice could last longest. The effect of this eating back into the slopes also gives us another very characteristic feature, the sharp two-sloped ridge, or the strip of remaining rounded hill running between two steep slopes.

Darwin also mentions perched boulders, and these too form a distinguishing feature of the upland area. They stand in places to which they could not have fallen, often precariously perched as if about to tumble down the slope, thus proving that they have not rolled there either as any momentum would have carried them on. These have been simply dropped where they now are by the melting ice, having been carried on its surface (if

Llyn Eigiau

they are sharp-edged) or if they are rounded in or underneath it.

The lakes themselves vary quite surprisingly in depth. The shallowest is Ogwen, which nowhere reaches more than ten feet. Eigiau and Idwal are surprisingly shallow too. The deepest is Cowlyd, which has been recorded at 222 feet, followed by Llydaw at 190, Dulyn 189 and Glaslyn at 127. In long historical terms all our lakes may be seen as being in the process of silting. A large area of marsh at the head of Llyn Eigiau shows us this process taking place, the lake once having occupied all this area; and at Llyn Ogwen we can see a promontory forming from the silt carried down from the slopes of Glyder Fawr by the rushing stream which drains Cwm Bochlwyd. The lake which once undoubtedly lay at the bottom of Nant Ffrancon is now completely silted, and may be seen as a large basin of marshy ground.

Thus we can see, with our own eyes, that the landscape is in motion. The time-scale, measured against human lives, is immense, but one thing we can also see is that it is speeding up. When we dealt early in the chapter with geological time, the time it took for the rocks themselves to form, we were talking about hundreds of millions of years. When we came to glacial time we have to think only in tens of thousands. The greatest of the successive ice ages occurred some 18,000 years ago, the earliest about 26,000, and by 10,000 years ago the ice had gone. Since then the rivers have continued to carry silt towards the sea, gradually wearing away the mountains.

The speed of change has been increased, of course, by our own arrival. Clearing the uplands and then the valleys for agriculture we have encouraged the process of erosion, further increased by the denuding of the slopes by sheep. It is only vegetation which holds the soil in place, and where the sheep, over the last two centuries, have stripped it we can see the bones of the mountain becoming increasingly visible. With the top soil gone the vegetation cannot return, and erosion takes place so much the faster.

A standing stone at Bwlch y Ddeufaen above the Conwy valley

Upland Habitations

At the height of two thousand five hundred feet in the Carneddau lies a plateau of solid peat many feet thick. Analysis of the pollen found in such upland peat beds in this area has shown that the land at this height was once clothed in alder, birch and hazel. Today these would not grow much above eight hundred feet. They flourished at two thousand feet in the post-glacial period known as Boreal, from 7000 to 5500 B.C., when the climate was warm and fairly dry, and were succeeded in slightly wetter (but still warm) times by alder and oak, in a period known as Atlantic. This ended in about 2000 B.C., and before that time the only open ground in North Wales was along the coast, on exposed headlands where the forest was thinned by the salt wind.

This was the situation when human beings first penetrated our area. If you look at a map of neolithic structures, which started to be built here in about 2500 B.C., you will see that they strikingly cling to the coast. It is only in the drier weather of the Sub-Boreal period, from 2000 B.C. to about 700, that a difference in the climate began to thin the forest at its upper edges and made the establishment of flocks feasible.

Climate has always governed human settlement and activity, and if we think we are undergoing a climate change at present we should simply bear in mind that this is nothing new. There have been vast swings of change before. Human activity may accelerate a process which is taking place, and the introduction of flocks of sheep and goats during the Sub-Boreal period prevented the forest from recurring in the uplands just as in cooler and drier times the tree-line was declining. The population of the hills was thus enabled to expand.

Cairns and perhaps stone circles are products of the Bronze Age, and both may be found very widely scattered and in great numbers in the mountain area. The Bronze Age cairns may be found both on hill summits and on low and level ground, some, as that on the summit of Moel Hebog, at over 2000 feet, and those which form the summit cairns of Carnedd Dafydd, Carnedd Llywelyn and Foel Grach at over three. These are burial mounds. Where they have not been anciently robbed the occasional successful excavation has revealed a central cell containing a cremation in an urn. They do not indicate the existence of habitations at these considerable heights, and indeed none has been found. The location of the dwellings of the Bronze Age people is a

Druid's Circle above Penmaenmawr

A prehistoric cairn at Bwlch y Ddeufaen

continuing puzzle, since the frequency of their burial cairns and mounds, together with their very considerable activity at the copper mines of the Great Orme indicates that they must have been numerous. There is the possibility that a complex of hut circles and compounds in the valley below Llyn Dulyn, north-east of Carnedd Llywelyn, may be Bronze Age, but even if this were proved it would account for only a fraction of the population which must have lived in this area at that time.

Just as the Great Orme copper mines undoubtedly occupied many people during the Bronze Age, so at an even earlier point did the stone axe factory on Penmaenmawr, at the extreme north of the mountain area. This extended, at its peak, over a distance of two miles, and seems to have been in use for several hundred years. It is now, unfortunately, largely destroyed by the quarry, but was fairly thoroughly investigated before it went. Axes of several types were produced, for light local use and for export for forest clearance. Since they have been found as far away as Cornwall and Northern Ireland the enterprise, in about 2500 B.C., implies trade, as does the copper production some seven hundred years later, and trade in turn implies political organisation. It would clearly be wrong to underestimate our prehistoric predecessors.

The pattern of vegetation in Snowdonian valley during the post-glacial period, which takes us into observable times, has varied slightly with changes in climate which controlled the height of the line at which trees would grow on the upland slopes, and this in turn was what originally decided where the first human settlements would occur. At those times when the tree line was highest the weather would of course have been milder, so that occupation of the hills was practicable at much greater heights then than it is today. The deep peat deposits at 2750 feet above sea level on the plateau above Cwm Eigiau, for instance, (693659), show quite clearly that for much of the period of prehistory almost the whole of the area we are considering would have been covered by thick undergrowth and, lower down, dense forest. It was for this reason that the very early settlements tended to take place not here in the valley but on coastal promontories where the salt air discouraged the growth of trees.

There are some superb examples in Snowdonia of the oldest of all man-made structures in Britain, the megalithic chamber tombs. A very fine and well-preserved one, known as Maen-y-Bardd, *the Bard's Stone*, stands beside

Capel Garmon Cromlech

Cromlech Maen y Bardd, Ro-wen

the Roman road above Ro-wen, (740718). Though not as large as some elsewhere, it possesses such firm proportions and such a lofty stance on the mountain's flank that it bears an unmatched air of nobility. Being in very much its original state it also illustrates the principles of construction of these neolithic burial chambers, by which a large capstone is poised on four or five uprights.

The tombs were originally covered over with a mound of earth and small stones, though it is not certain that the mound at Maen-y-Bardd was ever completed. A more elaborate example of a chamber tomb in this area, in which the mound is in place, occurs at Capel Garmon, above the eastern valley slope (819543). Here one can see a tomb consisting of not one but three linked chambers, a passage leading into them, and a long oblong concealing mound. Once again a superb outlook over largely unchanged landscape gives a sense of timelessness. From both sites the limit of the present treeline indicates the level below which, for these late-Stone-Age builders, the valley would have effectively uninhabitable.

Although the tomb at Capel Garmon has been excavated, its treatment over the intervening ages had destroyed most of its original remains, and only small pieces of bone and pottery were found. These however are sufficient to date it about 2500 B.C., which is consistent with similar tombs elsewhere, and to indicate that its use continued from neolithic into Bronze Age times.

There are no less than six chambered tombs within a five-mile radius in the area of Harlech. The tombs here are of the 'portal' type, best examined perhaps in the two very fine examples which lie behind the school at Dyffryn Ardudwy.

Now two separate chambers, these are still surrounded by the remains of the vast mound of stones which originally united them in a single monument. The form, once one looks for it, is clear. A pair of uprights slightly higher than the others forms what appears to be a doorway at the eastern end of the chamber, their flat sides facing each other; a universal characteristic of this feature is that the apparent doorway is then blocked, in a way which must have been permanent and intrinsic to the design, by a slightly lower stone set across the gap between them to form the cross-piece, on a plan, of the letter H. Since this feature means that the portal cannot have been used as such, its nature must be symbolic or conventional. A result of the greater

Carneddi Hengwm above Harlech

*Cromlechi at Corsygedol and
Dyffryn Ardudwy*

height of the portal stones is that the capstone slopes downwards slightly towards the west.

The capstones are normally smooth and flat underneath, but rounded and rough on top, suggesting perhaps that their underside was intended to be seen, by people entering the tomb, but that their exterior would have been covered. Indeed the tombs were always intended to be built over by a mound of stones, and the extent of such a covering can be seen in the Dyffryn example. The great field enclosures of the 19th century led to an enormous amount of wall-building, as may be plainly seen on the slopes and foothills around, and we know by comparing 18th-century descriptions and drawings with what may now be seen that a large quantity of the covering stones has in most instances been removed.

The fact that we do not know where the people who built these monuments lived may be due simply to the slightness of their dwellings, in a warm climate free, apparently, of the need for defensive structures. We know a little about their lives, however, from the things they made, some samples of their artefacts having been clearly identified. Some urns and a number of swords and daggers were found at Beddgelert, and a magnificent shield on the slopes of Moel Siabod.

If we know a great deal more about the people of the next phase of our history, the Iron Age, it is because they built substantial defensive citadels. We know from this at least that they had the need to, and so must envisage a society based on the idea of territory and hence both politically organised and settled. Once again we find their hillforts occurring mainly in connection with the coast, but here there are exceptions.

The first defences at Dinas Emrys, below the lakes in the Gwynant valley below Snowdon seem to have been from the first or second century, and there are signs of early Iron Age use. A defended hill also occurs at Dinas, further down that valley below Llyn Dinas, and in the same area there is a substantial small fort on Pen y Gaer, beside the Aberglaslyn pass. All of this indicates that the mountains were penetrated up this valley at an early period. Two other small forts occur at the edge of the upland area above the coastal plain near where the river Dwyfor emerges from the hills at Dolbenmaen. And at Llanberis a small fort, now much damaged, occurs directly above the back of the town. Otherwise there is little to indicate that the hill-fort building tribes inhabited the upland area.

*Bwlch Tyddiad – the prehistoric track the old track known as
'Roman Steps' above Cwm Bychan, Harlech*

Things are very different when we consider the evidently more peaceable early remains. Hut and enclosures associated, in some cases, with field systems crowd the foothills and creep into the uplands, making it clear that by the time the Romans came (to which period some of them have been dated) the hills, except for the barest summits, were being fairly intensively farmed.

Since this form of dwelling, known as the round hut, was clearly in use over a considerable period we cannot allocate the remains in general to any particular phase. Rather we may say that it spans the whole of our early history, from the time of the coming of the Iron Age tribes in the first thousand years B.C., perhaps before that, through the Roman period (here in the hills probably largely undisturbed by that) and out again into the Dark Ages and early medieval times.

Sometimes the huts occur singly, sometimes in groups; sometimes the groups are within an enclosure, though this is evidently more an agricultural compound than a defensive work. Certainly they also occur within the hillforts, sometimes clearly contemporary with them, at others possibly indicating an afteruse of the ramparts for containing cattle rather than keeping out enemies. The actual form is a simple one, and easily recognised, since it is a ring of stones embedded in the earth. This formed the foundation of a wigwam-type construction made of birch or alder boughs and roofed with peat or thatch. Destructible but endlessly replaceable, the form is adaptable to either permanent settlement or seasonal migration.

The best examples in our area occur at high levels and so are rather inaccessible. This does not necessarily indicate a pattern of distribution, since any ancient structure would be vulnerable at lower levels to destruction by agriculture and in the building of walls; but the climatic factors we mentioned at the start of the chapter are relevant, since it was comfortable to live, and more convenient to farm, at heights of over a thousand feet in earlier times.

Tomen y Mur

A New Order Arrives

If you take the road across the neck of the Llŷn peninsula from Caernarfon to Porthmadog you will find that the familiar twisting Welsh lane becomes, either side of Dolbenmaen, startlingly straight. Experience leads me to suspect the imposition on our haphazard countryside of imperial order. Sure enough there was discovered, in the course of excavation of a gravel pit, a small Roman fort near to the site of the former railway station at Bryncir, a mile or so from Dolbenmaen. It had at least two barrack blocks, and was occupied during the first century A.D. Nothing of it now remains to be seen, but its existence marks the furthest west the Romans appear to have settled on the mainland in North Wales.

The camp at Dolbenmaen may have been a posting point on the route between the major fort of Segontium at Caernarfon, and the auxiliary outpost at Tomen y Mur. The latter is of some importance, since it was the point at which the road from Segontium and that from Canovium in the Conwy valley joined up on their route southwards to the South Wales centre Moridunum, now Carmarthen.

At Tomen y Mur there are extensive remains to be seen, now mainly in the form of grass banks, including the area of an amphitheatre, a little way from the main fort. The most conspicuous feature is the mound or 'tomen' which gives the place its name, thought to be the motte of a medieval castle, which would have been a wooden structure on its top, probably built by an English earl attempting invasion. The most striking quality of the site is its extreme exposure, a bleakness and lack of shelter which must have tested the hardiness of its Roman garrison.

That the legions went through the mountains as well as round them is proved by the existence of a marching camp at Penygwryd, at the junction of the Llanberis and Nant Gwynant passes and on the route to Capel Curig and so a link, as we shall see, to the main north-south route. This indicates that the mountain passes were used as well by the Romans, which in turn suggests much more of a network of communications in North Wales than the evidence on the ground by itself has so far shown. Only traces of early, possibly Roman, roads have been found in the central uplands, one at Penygwryd in fact said to be later than the camp and lost, in any case, under the modern road.

*Segontium – the Roman fort
at Caernarfon*

Caer Llugwy at Capel Curig

It must be said as well that there is nothing to be seen in the way of Roman ruins at Penygwryd now. Only a possible indication of a wall in the form of a bank in the field running down to the road as it sets off down to Nant Gwynant may show the outline of the fort. The hotel lies on its northern border, and the whole embraces the road junction and the start of the two southerly forks. The east side of the fort is now submerged in the artificial lake.

If a road ran to Caernarfon this way, it left the main Roman road in the area at Caer Llugwy, otherwise known as Bryn y Gefeiliau. Here, for once, there is something to see, in the form of recognisable banks in a field where the walls of the fort once stood. You can even see in places the stone bases of the walls.

The existence of Caer Llugwy had long been suspected, and could anyway have been inferred because (like the outpost at Dolbenmaen probably on one route from Caernarfon to Trawsfynydd) it lay at the right distance to be a posting-point from the fort in the Conwy valley, Canovium, now Caerhun. Ancient Roman ruins on the river Llugwy had been known about and then forgotten, but in the 1920's the site was properly excavated.

To find Caer Llugwy you take the old coaching road which deviates from the present A5 just as it crosses the Llugwy river, about half way from Betws-y-coed to Capel Curig. The fort lies between the road and the river, at a point where the latter does a big loop away from the road and back. This loop encloses the Roman fort. Its form in the usual rigid rectangle. Excavations have indicated that it was in use between 90 and 140 A.D.

The presence of Caer Llugwy at this particular spot tells us something about the route of the great Roman road known as Sarn Helen, which, it is known, ran from Canovium to Trawsfynydd and thence south to the main Roman town in Wales, Maridunum, now Carmarthen. A stretch of this is clearly identifiable in this area, where it runs across the uplands from the top of Betws-y-coed down to Pont-y-pant in the Lledr valley. This would lead us to expect that it followed the west bank of the Conwy valley until it met the Llugwy. The posting fort would then have been at Betws, and its presence a couple of miles upstream means that for a time at least there was another route taking higher ground from Canovium to drop to this point, then perhaps running downstream to the known part of Sarn Helen at Betws.

It hardly needs to be repeated that a main feature of the Roman military

Canovium – the present churchyard wall at Caerhun above the Conwy river crossing follows the line of the outer wall of the old Roman fort

Canovium

technique was this establishment of permanent lines of communication between the main occupied forts. In many parts of Britain these roads set the form of the future network, and are there still under our modern roads. In this area we are lucky to be able to see them in two instances unmodified, one being the stretch of Sarn Helen between Betws and Pont-y-pant already mentioned. The other is the connection from Canovium in the Conwy valley to Segontium at Caernarfon.

This runs across the hills between Tal y Fan and Drum, through a pass known as Bwlch y Ddeufaen, the pass of the two stones (after the magnificent standing stones which so clearly identify it) and falls to the coast at Aber. It is probably one of the first Roman routes to be established, since invasion of Anglesey was an early priority. It was, Tacitus tells us, 'feeding the national resistance'. Hence in 61 A.D. Suetonius Paulinus set out from a base in Chester to march through North Wales and conquer Anglesey. To do so he had to establish the fort on the crossing of the Conwy river, and from it this route across the hills. It was then used again in 77 by Agricola, on his more forceful and more successful expedition into North Wales, when the forts at either end of it took a more permanent form.

That we have even these two pieces of road is perhaps surprising, and the lack of more than fragments of the probable connecting roads may be explained. Substantial road building did not take place in Britain as a whole until the time of Hadrian, who came to Britain in 122 A.D. But at that time Roman interest in Wales decreased, as pressure increased in the north of Britain. With Wales for the time being reasonably settled the two main forts here had their garrisons severely cut at the time when manpower from all over Britain was concentrated on the building of Hadrian's wall, in the 120's. It thus seems likely that the road-building programme in North Wales was left unfinished, which is why only short stretches of the intermediate roads have been found.

We are able to put a date to the period when the roads were in use through the lucky discovery of fully datable Roman milestones. One, on the northern plain below the foothills lies on the evident route of the road from Canovium to Segontium, and dates from the time of the emperor Marcus Aurelius. Another on the same route but further west is from the time of Trajan. Above Llanfairfechan on the northern slopes, not one but two stones, found ten yards apart, marked presumably a revision in the route the road took coming

Roman Road at Bwlch y Ddeufaen

down from Bwlch y Ddeufaen. These, found in 1833, are now in the British Museum. The earlier of the two records the eighth mile from Canovium and commemorates the year 121 A.D., that of Hadrian's visit to Britain. The second dates from between 207 and 209, the time of Septimus Severus.

Though other signs of the Roman presence have been found – such as a minor earthwork near the route of the road approaching Segontium, and a bath-house just west of Tremadog – there is nothing to see of them today, and the main impact of their occupation seems to have been confined to the network of roads and forts which they spread around the central mountain block. By simply marching through it they hardly affected it at all. The inhabitants continued to live independent lives in their round huts (there is no sign of the introduction of the square Roman form, or of the villa-homestead with which more hospitable parts of Britain were dotted), and indeed one may speculate that if the Roman presence was noticeable to them at all it was as something of a convenience as a protection against other invaders and the source of a settled and stable way of life. Great military engagements meanwhile took place elsewhere. Here in the hills the absence of interference let a way of life continue which, with its associated culture, flowed naturally from the pre-Roman Iron Age to the post-Roman Dark Ages.

Dinas Emrys
insert: remains of man-made
pool at the summit

Refuge of Princes

Partly because of its security, the heartland of North Wales has from time to time had a role to play in the country's history. Indeed if any particular spot could be regarded as central to Wales' identity, it must be Dinas Emrys.

Because it lies at the foot of the Snowdon massif itself and overlooking the junction of the Nant Gwynant pass with the descent to the Aberglaslyn, Dinas Emrys is in a highly defined position geographically, and this is matched by its position in history and culture. There are signs (as mentioned in an earlier chapter) that it was in use from before Roman times and into them, and it was certainly occupied shortly after that; a substantial settlement had arisen there by the second half of the fifth century.

Dinas Emrys occurs in one of our earliest literary sources, the 'History of the Brython' by a Welsh priest called Nennius, who wrote about 800 A.D. Here (with some support from the Anglo-Saxon Chronicle) we can discern what actually happened in the sixth century. The king of Britain, named as Vortigern (which scholars now think was more of a title, 'High King', than a name) was in trouble with the Germanic tribes he had allowed to settle as mercenaries: in exchange for provisions they supported him against the Picts and the Irish, who were causing problems after the Roman withdrawal. The Germans brought their families over, and as their numbers increased he was unable to keep up the provisions. As they took control his advisers told him to withdraw to a fortifiable place. ' . . . and at last they came to the country called Gwynedd; and when he was exploring in the mountains of Eryri, that is, in English, Snowdon, he at length reached a place in one of the mountains that was suitable for building a stronghold'. Later in the story we hear how the hilltop came to be called after Emrys, the Brythonic form of the Roman name Ambrosius. The tale forms, in fact, something of a sequel to the story of Lludd and Llefelys in the Mabinogion, where it is said of the location of the events 'the form by which that place was known thereafter was Dinas Emrys'.

The web of story surrounding Dinas Emrys is complex, and in fact occupies a full chapter in my book 'Gods and Heroes in North Wales'. Vortigern, on arriving, failed to build his citadel, and was told by his wise men to sacrifice a child who had no father. Such a child was found, and turned out to be Ambrosius, in history the Brythonic leader who rallied resistance after Vortigern's failure. In the story he acts the role later filled by

The Red Dragon of Wales

Dinas Emrys

Merlin (a character adapted from this same story by Geoffrey of Monmouth), the prophet who foretells the future of Britain. He tells the wise men that there are dragons buried there (and the story of Lludd and Llefelys in fact tells us how this came about), and when this proved correct there occurs the famous image of the dragons fighting, the white (representing the Saxons) driving out the red, the Brythonic dragon, which, however, will eventually recover and win. The red dragon had been a particularly North Wales element since the seventh century, when it was the battle standard of King Cadwaladr; Henry Tudor, his remote descendant, flew it as his personal standard at the Battle of Bosworth. Meanwhile it had been adopted as the symbol of Wales as a whole, and when the the Black Prince, as Prince of Wales, fought at the battle of Crecy he and his Welsh troops rallied to that banner. It is interesting, standing on Dinas Emrys today, to think that this is precisely the spot where the symbolism arose.

When Dr Savoury of the National Museum of Wales excavated this hilltop in the 1950's he found some evidence of the origins of the legend. There was an early-Roman period man-made pool on the hill's summit, where the dragons were said to be buried; and over part of it was a Dark Age period paved platform. A flourishing community lived there in the time of Vortigern and Ambrosius, the mid fifth century. A later lord evidently took refuge there as well, since the only clear sign of occupation there now is the keep of a 13th century castle, about which nothing more is known. The hill is now in the hands of the National Trust.

Although (as the story recognises) most of the island of Britain became in due course occupied by Germanic tribes, the heartland into which Vortigern retreated and from which Ambrosius rallied remained independent and free long after the Anglo-Saxons themselves, in the rest of Britain, had become subject to the rule of the Norman French. Attempts by the Normans to complete their conquest by subduing Wales came up against the barrier of this inner heartland, which, not surprisingly, they failed to penetrate. There are thus Welsh castles here rather than Norman ones (and that on the summit of Dinas Emrys is likely to be such).

During this time of independence North Wales had a highly-structured political system, within which both artistic culture and religion flourished. The prince had a court in each district, and moved between them. At Dolbenmaen, for instance, there is a motte, now surrounded by ruined farm

Dolwyddelan castle – a stronghold of the Welsh princes

Dolbadarn castle in the heart of Eryri

buildings and clothed in trees, which was once the castle from which the district of Eifionydd was ruled, which later moved down the river Dwyryd to Cricieth. Earth-work and timber castles such as this were superceded in the 13th century by stone-built structures, and a fine example of one of these stands beside the Padarn lake.

For much of that time Llywelyn the Great ruled much of Wales. Traditionally Llywelyn is said to have been born at Dolwyddelan, but if this is true it is unlikely to have been in the present castle. He was born in the 1170's, and the earliest parts of the castle seem to belong to the early decades of the next century. Across the road below the castle, however, is a natural hillock, now tree-topped, on which an earlier castle stood. It is possible that this one was the North Wales home of Llywelyn's father, Iorwerth.

It is in fact likely that the first version of the present castle was built by Llywelyn himself. Its firmly rectangular tower marks it as early work, before Llywelyn developed the new fashion for d-shaped and finally round keeps.

It is clear that in fact he mixed the two styles, during his period of castle-building. At Cricieth there is a rectangular tower of the same size as that at Dolwyddelan, and at Castell y Bere, south of Dolgellau, which Llywelyn built after his seizing of Meirionnydd from his son Gruffudd in 1221, there are examples of all three forms, the rectangular keep in the middle being the same size as that at Dolwyddelan.

Dolbadarn Castle was built by Llywelyn the Great in the late 1220's or early 1230's, not at the site of one of his courts which controlled the 'commotes' or administrative districts, but rather on a line of travel between them. It defends the route through the hills via the Llanberis pass, just as Llywelyn's other main castle at Dolwyddelan controlled another traverse of the mountains through the Lledr valley. Although Llywelyn had done much to unify Wales, and was a force to be reckoned with by the English crown, the presence of these castles reminds us that his position was never secure. The stronger the Welsh princes were, the more they were surrounded by the resentment of the displaced. Indeed Dolbadarn castle is famous for having been (according to Leland, in the 16th century), the place of imprisonment for some twenty-two years of Owain, the defeated brother of Llywelyn ap Gruffudd, who, like his grandfather Llywelyn the Great, had fought his nearest relatives to gain the princedom.

As well as being unusual for its time in having a round rather than a

Bwthyn Llywelyn, the National Trust property in Beddgelert

Cymer Abbey near Dolgellau

square tower, the new form which was being developed by the Normans along the border at this period, Dolbadarn is unusual too for having three floors, rather than the usual two.

The keep which you see at the moment is only the best remaining part of a more extensive defensive layout. Closer inspection will show the hill on which it stands to have been surrounded by a curtain wall (once some ten feet high, now reduced to less than three), within which once stood a hall, a tower to the west, another building on the eastern side, all grouped around a courtyard.

Llywelyn almost certainly had a court at Beddgelert, where the story of the faithful hound (an international popular tale with no special Welsh connection) became attached to his name. 'Gelert's grave' is now perhaps the little town's best-known feature, but is of course entirely spurious. The name Beddgelert does in fact mean the burial place of Gelert, but he was the founding saint of the parish, not a dog. The story of the hound was introduced by the landlord of the Goat Hotel, a Mr David Pritchard, towards the end of the eighteenth century. He it was also who provided the village with the grave, an enterprising piece of tourism management which has certainly paid off. It makes the point that people greatly prefer fiction to fact.

'Llywelyn's cottage' is a late 17th century building, but may of course stand on the site of his court. There is a monastic connection which makes it seem likely that he would reside here when in this area, since the surrounding land had been granted by him to the Abbey of Aberconwy in about 1200, to which he had given its original charter and where he also had a residence. Llywelyn's keen interest in monastic foundations is amply proved, and this area would have appealed to him since there was a priory here from very early times.

Llywelyn the Great sponsored the foundation of a major Cistercian abbey, that of Cymer, the ruins of which lie in a still tranquil setting hard by the murmuring river Mawddach. The Cistercians favoured locations remote from other settlements, which this remarkably remains. Destroyed at the Dissolution, not much survives of what was evidently quite a large complex; yet the substantial arches of the ruin and the elegant tall lancet windows in one remaining wall gives clues of a degree of splendour.

It was because it was normally impossible for enemies to cross the Conwy, with the Welsh defending its western bank, that Llywelyn and his descendant Llywelyn ap Gruffudd were able to have one of their main courts at Aber, on

Pen y Bryn, Abergwyngregyn

Abergwyngregyn

The Motte at Abergwyngregyn

Archaeological research at Abergwyngregyn, 2011

the northern coast. It might be worth noting here that whenever the place is named in the Welsh chronicles the name of it is 'Aber': 'bu varw Dam Siwan, verch Ieuan vrenhin . . . yn llys Aber', and so on. Our historic sources, Leland, Pennant, Byng, Fenton, all knew it by that name. In modern times the historians Bezant Lowe, the compilers of the Royal Commission on Ancient Monuments Inventory, Professor Dodd, H.R. Davies and John Davies all call it Aber. Whatever justification there may be for the recent imposition of the name Abergwyngregyn, there is none in the historical sources.

The Chronicles note that Llywelyn's beloved wife Joan, daughter of King John, died at his court at Aber; and later that his son Dafydd died there too. Since it was also the place from which his successor Llywelyn ap Gruffudd negotiated with Edward I we might be justified in supposing that this, among all the courts of the independent princes, was one of the most important.

The location of Llywelyn's court at Aber is a matter of dispute. It is often supposed, following Leland, that the motte known as Pen y Mwd forms the site, since he says some of the building still stood there in his time. Pen y Mwd is a round twenty-two foot high earthwork close to the river. In style it is recognisable as the motte of a Norman Motte-and-bailey castle, with no sign of the bailey, and so would have been likely to be of the period immediately preceding Llywelyn's castle building. It must be said firstly that the sites of Llywelyn's courts (as opposed to his castles) are often not known, an argument for supposing that they did not normally involve mottes; and that this is confirmed in the two cases where sites of his courts have been identified and thoroughly investigated, at Llanfaes and at Rhosyr in Anglesey. These would have us to suppose that somewhere under the turf of Aber there are stone foundations of substantial buildings.

Sure enough, near the motte archeological investigations in 1993 and 2010 have revealed the foundations of a considerable stone building of the 14th century, possibly dating from the period shortly after the Edwardian invasion, and so perhaps on the site of the *Llys* of the independent princes. If so, then this was the place at which both the wife and son of Llywelyn the Great died.

The Conwy valley also has the honour of having close connections with this great statesman. Llywelyn is said to have built himself a residence – probably a hunting court – at Trefriw, in the heart of the valley, where tradition claims that he founded the parish church. Before that was built, it

Llanrhychwyn church, above Trefriw in the Conwy valley, known as 'Llywelyn's old church'

is said, he and his wife Joan (the natural daughter of King John) used to walk up the steep track to the older church of Llanrhychwyn (774616). Legend says he built the church in the valley to save his wife the effort of this walk.

Anyone coming up to Llanrhychwyn today enters at once that pure ancient world of the Middle Ages in which Llywelyn lived. The building is squat, sturdy and simple, sheltered by magnificent yews. The country around is upland farmland, at the point at which the valley slopes break into a plateau of mountain pasture, the tree-line fragmenting, the sky broadening, the air sharpening with mountain freshness. 'The old church of Llywelyn', as it is sometimes called, still in occasional use, is in character with this terrain.

The oldest part, perhaps built in the 12th century, is the wall and neighbouring corner around the doorway. The font ahead of the entry is probably also of this date. The church was lengthened and the chancel added probably in the 15th century, and the north aisle added in the early 16th. Another ancient mountain church may be seen above Henryd, that of Llangelynnin (751737). Here too a simple medieval building (now the western nave) was extended by the addition of the present chancel in the 15th century.

Llywelyn was a devotedly religious man, and among the historic acts for which he found time was the foundation of the Abbey of Aberconwy, the first settlement where Conwy now stands, to which he gave a charter in 1189. No doubt he was a frequent visitor to the monastery there, and it is appropriate that it was there that he died and was buried, in the year 1240.

The relative stability which Llywelyn had achieved was not to last, and the war between his grandson, Llywelyn ap Gruffudd, and King John's grandson, Edward I, culminated in a massive invasion of North Wales in 1282. Dolwyddelan castle, which the last prince had made his headquarters, fell to the English in January 1283, enabling Edward to march down the western side of the Conwy valley and control the crossing place at Conwy.

In order to build his famous garrison town there, the king first had to move the occupants, the monks of Llywelyn's Cistercian Abbey. He gave them new territory in the valley, and transported the monastery wholesale to Maenan (789658) where it remained until the Dissolution of the Monasteries. Very little may be seen of it there now, only a few foundation stones in the grounds of the Maenan Abbey Hotel. The monks took with them, however, the coffin of their patron, enclosed in a magnificent stone sarcophagus. After the Dissolution this disappeared, and only the rediscovered bottom half of the

Tŵr Llywelyn Conwy and Llywelyn's memorial in the town square

stone casing may now be seen, housed in the Wynn chapel at the old church of Llanrwst (798616), in which church is also preserved the Abbey's magnificently carved rood-screen. It is not known where is the final resting-place of the remains of Llywelyn Fawr.

Llywelyn's stone cask in Llanrwst church

*Harlech castle against the
splendid backdrop of Eryri*

Harlech

Edward and Llywelyn ap Gruffudd (Llywelyn Fawr's grandson) had started their conflict in the border country in 1277, and the tension between them reached a climax when the Welsh prince and his brother led raids on the Marches in the spring of 1282, thus breaking the rather fragile agreement which had been contrived between the two countries. Llywelyn died in a skirmish in mid-Wales at the end of that year, and Edward took advantage of the temporary confusion to launch an all-out invasion of Gwynedd, the heartland and refuge of the independent princes. He threw round the inner sanctuary of Snowdonia a great chain of castles.

The southernmost of these is Harlech.

Since the site of Harlech castle occurs in the mythology, it is possible that this notably prominent rock was a sacred or defensive position before Edward came; but it must be said that there is no evidence of this. Harlech as we have it was one of the castles designed for Edward from scratch by Master James of St George, a Frenchman who had supervised the building of castles in Edward's other territories, and who accompanied him into Wales as master of his works there.

That Master James was a genius in his own field is clearly evident to us today. Each of Edward's North Wales castles bears its own unique style and character; yet each conforms to a rigid overall form demanded by its serious military function. Each one bears touches of symmetry and harmony, and even overt decoration, which makes it individually beautiful. Yet they all worked effectively as formidable tools of war. They are variations on a grandiose theme.

Harlech is undoubtedly the most intimate and domestic of the main three. Caernarfon is palatial and grand, Conwy somewhat intimidating in its aspect of power. Harlech is impressive from the outside, due to its splendid eminence, but in its interior it is the sort of place where one feels one could comfortably live. The great windows of its inner face look onto a securely enclosed court, giving rather the feel of a fortified manor, an atmosphere which comes as all the more of a surprise after the view of it rearing against the sky as one approaches.

Edward sited his castles with the eye of a strategist, a day's march apart and in such positions as could be supplied by sea, from his headquarters at

Chester, if land communications were cut off. In view of this it is important to remember, at Harlech, that the coastline has changed, this time the land gaining from the sea. Indeed as one stands on the edge of the outer ward it is surprising that so much change could happen in the relatively short period of seven hundred years. This is thought to be partly due to the change of course of the river Dwyryd, which now meets the sea in a combined estuary with the Glaslyn some four miles further north. If the outflow of that river at that time skirted the foot of the castle rock, then Edward's harbour might well have been on that, rather than on the seashore. Certainly the Water-Gate, and the path to the castle known as 'the way from the sea' emphasise, even today, Harlech's maritime role.

Although Harlech was built at the same time as Conwy and Caernarfon, we can see a development in style taking place which was to lead, a few years later, to the fully concentric form of Beaumaris. Harlech is in a transitional position between the older form of inner and outer wards, (developed from the keep and bailey fortresses of the earlier Middle Ages), on the one hand, in which the inner citadel is approached through the outer, and on the other the doubling-up effect displayed at Beaumaris, in which the outer ward completely encircles the inner. One can see Master James approaching this later idea at Harlech.

Once there, the castle attracted its own history. It was finished in about 1290, and immediately tested in the revolt of Madog ap Llywelyn in 1294-5. Although besieged by land, it proved the effectiveness of its water-based position, and the garrison held out against the rebels by receiving supplies by sea. Cricieth castle, refortified by Edward, proved equally effective in his service.

For a time there was peace, the system set up by Edward effectively ruling

Wales. The death of Richard II in 1399 and the usurpation of the throne by Henry IV, however, led to a less settled situation. It was due to a dispute with a neighbour that Owain Glyndŵr found himself out of favour with the new king, and forced into the role of rebel. But evidently the time was ripe for rebellion, and all that had been lacking was a leader.

The Owain Glyndŵr War erupted in 1400 when the whole nation rose in arms against the colonial towns and castles that were the focus of the Norman and English occupation in Wales. The leader, Glyndŵr, was a baron with border estates at Glyndyfrdwy and Sycharth, who also inherited royal blood from the main three lines of Welsh princes. He was proclaimed Prince of Wales before the first attacks on Ruthin, Denbigh, Flint, Holt, Rhuddlan, Oswestry and Welshpool. Henry IV of England immediately retaliated by passing Penal Laws against the Welsh, further constricting their rights in their own lands – laws recognised by historians as the most racial in medieval Europe. The Owain Glyndŵr War became a cause for national survival and was supported by bishops and clergy, abbots and monks, scholars and lawyers, gentry and commoners.

By 1402 Glyndŵr's forces had seen widespread action throughout the country, and gained a famous victory at Bryn Glas near the Hereford border. English settlements were burned and castles be sieged. Henry IV sent armies to try and capture Owain, but his heavy horses and war machinery were too slow for the Welsh guerilla forces. Owain was a Scarlet Pimpernel, emerging from mountain mists, striking a blow and then disappearing. One moment Harlech was under his siege and 500 men were sent from Chester to save the castle; the next moment Owain and his army were attacking Caernarfon town and castle. All Henry could do was burn abbeys and towns that supported Owain and catch a few rebels and hang them – further fuelling the flames of revolt.

Henry's armies returned empty handed to Hereford or Shrewsbury but Owain's star was still rising. Substantial castles such as Conwy and Carmarthen fell to his hands for short periods and by 1403 he felt secure enough, with nearly the whole of Wales supporting him, that he held on to Aberystwyth and Harlech castles as his seats of power, with Harlech becoming his capital.

It was at Harlech that he showed that he was a political power as well as a guerilla leader. He built connections and sent ambassadors to Ireland,

Heritage boards with details of Owain Glyndŵr's great seal and coat of arms and the main events of his war

Scotland and France and created a strong alliance with the king of France in particular, signing agreements and receiving military forces and equipment to help with his war against the English. Owain also entered the English political game of his age, taking advantage of severe rifts against the crown and signing a Tripartite Indenture with Henry Percy and Edmund Mortimer in 1405, splitting England and Wales between the three of them.

Owain convened at least two parliaments, with four representative from each commote in Wales attending. The first was held at Machynlleth in 1404 and another at Harlech in 1405. Wales was not represented at the London parliament until after 1536, and these assemblies were other steps towards fulfilling Owain's dream of creating a nation-state.

Owain Glyndŵr's vision of an independent church in Wales, with its own archbishop at St David's, and two universities to serve both north and south of the country, established him as 'the father of modern Wales'. His revolt was worn down by poverty and famine over the decade, but even when they lost Aberystwyth and Harlech castles in 1408-09, it was far from the end of the campaign. Owain is still highly regarded for his military strategy and guerilla tactics. Without obvious towers of strength to defend his army, he used the terrain of his country and the faithful following of his people to live an outlaw lifestyle until his death in 1415-1416. In parts of Eryri and Meirionnydd, the actual revolt itself extended over twelve years. As late as 1412, two substantial battalions were sent to Bala and Cymer to subdue the rekindling revolt in those areas. The final yield would have been the 600 strong gathering at Bala on 10 March, 1414, which took the oath to end the revolt.

Harlech became prominent again in Britain's next internal struggle, the long-drawn-out Wars of the Roses, when it was a Lancastrian stronghold, and indeed held out against the victorious Yorkists longer than any other fortress. It is to this period of siege and resistance that its famous song belongs, the tune of which is traditional and finds echoes in the anthems of other nations.

Medieval castles were the most sophisticated weapon of their time, but could not anticipate the innovations of later centuries, and their usefulness effectively ceased with the development of artillery. The power of gunpowder enabled the projecting of missiles over their high walls in constant bombardment, and the battering they received in these later times has left many of them in a much more ruined state than Harlech. In the Civil War of

Owain's motte at Glyndyfrdwy

*Owain's coat of arms at Llanrwst and
a Glyndŵr celebration at Twthill, Caernarfon*

the 17th century Harlech castle was defended for the King and besieged by Oliver Cromwell's brother-in-law, a local landowner called Colonel John Jones, who later came to be one of the signatories to the King's death-warrant. His ancestral home, Maes y Garnedd, may be seen at the very end of the lane which runs up the narrow Nantcol valley.

Harlech castle withstood the siege of Colonel Jones, but eventually it surrendered to the Parliamentary army under General Mytton, in 1647. Just as it had been the last of the Lancastrian castles in Britain to fall to the Yorkists, so it was the last castle to hold out for the King against Parliament, and the Civil War was over with its surrender. That event proved to be its last military act, and from then on it has been an unoccupied ruin.

You would not think that such a quiet place could have been involved in so much history. Harlech today has few notable buildings, and indeed it seems that it never had. Pennant, in the late 18th century, describes it as being 'a small and very poor town, remarkable only for its castle'. Speed's map of 1610 shows only a scattering of cottages some distance from the castle. It seems that Edward I did not establish there the borough which provided a garrison of English families to administer this government, as he did at Conwy and Caernarfon. Perhaps the reason is that he had created a borough already at Cricieth nearby, to which he may have hoped to entice the essential English colony to control this area.

The town which survives under the shadow of the castle now is pleasant and successful, still small enough to have an intimate and friendly atmosphere.

Owain Glyndŵr memorial at Corwen

Glyndŵr and the Aftermath

When the tides of war turned against Owain Glyndŵr, he lost possession of Harlech castle and his family were taken to the Tower of London and many of his men were killed. However, he did not give up the struggle – he went underground and continued fighting a guerilla campaign. Many stories grew up about his incredible ability to strike at the enemy and escape unscathed. He was transformed from being an historical hero to becoming a mythical figure. His death went unannounced and no one knows where he was buried. His son Maredudd continued to fight as an outlaw in Meirionnydd up until 1421 and Owain came to symbolise the unyielding spirit of independent Wales. Owain did not attend. He was hidden by his closest followers and the date of his death and even his grave is unknown. The poets did not sing one elegy in his memory. Owain moved from the history books into the heart of his people – he became the national hero of Wales and his dream lived on.

But Owain's war left its effect on Wales. Sir John Wynn, writing at the end of the sixteenth century, attributes the desolate state of much of North Wales, particularly the upper reaches of the Conwy valley, to depopulation caused by Owain's scorched-earth policy:

All the whole country then was but a forest, rough and spacious as it is still, but then waste of inhabitants and all overgrown with woods, for Owain Glyndŵr's wars, beginning in Anno 1400, continued fifteen years, which brought such a desolation . . . for it was Owain Glyndŵr's policy to bring all things to waste, that the English should find not strength nor resting-place in the country.

No doubt other factors, such as plague and disorder during the intervening period of the Wars of the Roses, were to blame as well. It is interesting to hear, however, that for one reason or another the moorland country around Penmachno and Dolwyddelan was a wasteland when, round about 1485, Sir John's great-grandfather moved his family up from Eifionydd to occupy Dolwyddelan castle. It was from here that the family moved on to the Conwy valley to create the Gwydir estate with its seat at Gwydir Castle, half a mile outside Llanrwst.

There is something in the style of the Wynn chapel at Llanrwst which contrasts with its parent body, that sound medieval parish church. It has a

Gwydir castle near Llanrwst, the Wynn family's estate

flare, an air of confident distinction. The explanation is simple: it is a true product of the Renaissance.

The effects of a new national attitude under the Tudor monarchy were not slow to reach Snowdonia, where a well-established local aristocracy lacked only the opportunity to take part in English affairs. When this was granted by the Act of Union of 1536, families such as the Wynns of Gwydir, the Gruffudds of Penrhyn and the Vaughans of Corsygedol, who were already great and powerful locally, were quick to export their ability and enterprise to London.

The chapel was built as a memorial to the greatness of the family by Sir Richard Wynn, the second baronet, in 1633. It is possible that Inigo Jones, then at the height of his career as a fashionable architect, who is thought to have had local connections and perhaps to have been a friend of the Wynn family, had a hand in its design. There is, however, unfortunately no certain evidence for this persistent tradition.

One cannot move in Llanrwst or its area without being aware of the influence of the Wynns. To get to the church by the river, for instance, you pass a line of almshouses which were founded by Sir John Wynn, the first baronet, to house twelve old men of the parish. Their simple elegance proclaims their period. It was in general a time of high quality. Today, these almshouses house the heritage museum of Llanrwst and its locality.

The most conspicuous feature is inevitably its bridge, the 'Pont Fawr' still splendidly in use in the late 20th century despite its great age. Its predecessor had fallen into 'the greatest decay' by the 1620s, and the two counties which it joined, Denbighshire and Caernarvonshire, between them raised the £1,000 necessary for its replacement, which was constructed in 1636. The legend that Inigo Jones designed it (along with the Wynn chapel) is so persistent as not to be ignored, and there is no doubt that Sir Richard would have had plenty of chance to get to know the great architect. Possibly he did a sketch for it while staying at Gwydir; but it must be said that there is no evidence, and the fact that the record of its origin – the demand for a new bridge, the raising of the money, and so on – makes no mention of this distinguished connection, rather indicates that it arose at a later date.

The bridge is steep enough now, but in early prints its slopes are even more precipitous, and it is known from the records that it was modified in the 1670's (when the central arch had collapsed) and again in 1702.

Since there was no other crossing place in the valley until the 19th century,

Gwydir Chapel at Llanrwst church

Llanrwst church and Wynn family memorial in Gwydir Chapel

the existence of this bridge made Llanrwst the hub of communications. As movement increased during the 17th and 18th centuries this factor became more important. An old house at one end of the bridge, Tu-hwnt-i'r-bont, 'beyond the bridge', which dates from the 17th century, and an old inn, Pen-y-bont, 'head of the bridge', at the other, show how the town formed at an early date around the river crossing. Llanrwst contains even today more than its share of well-established hostelries, and in early coaching times there would have been very many more.

To get a feeling of the power and stability of the Wynns one has to go to Gwydir itself, their family seat. The family was descended from the kings of Gwynedd, by a parallel line to that of Llywelyn Fawr. They bought the Gwydir estate from Llywelyn's great-grandson at the end of the 15th century. The Wynn family had originated in south-west Gwynedd, from where they moved to occupy Dolwyddelan castle in 1488. After the purchase of the estate the great-grandfather of the first baronet built the house at Gwydir.

It is a fine example of a Tudor country house, now unfortunately smaller by one wing than that occupied by Sir John, but still in good condition. It sits securely among protecting trees, one of which was planted to commemorate the wedding of Charles I. The interior contains some fine ceilings and panelling, and some of the windows and doorways appear to have been made from stone dressed for another purpose, presumably therefore retrieved from the demolished abbey at Maenan.

The family history of the Wynns was written by its most notable member, Sir John, who was among other things a competent historian. The reputation of the first baronet, however, is not otherwise as impeccable as would be appropriate to the high position of his family. Sir John was ruthless in his exploitation of tenants, to the extent that legal cases were brought against him by his more humane neighbours. Threatened with arrest, he used his family's connections at court to buy himself a pardon. His energetic pursuit of wealth enlarged the Wynn estate, and incidentally improved the Conwy valley. The mining of lead above Gwydir, workings of which can still be seen on the road up to Llyn Geirionydd, was one of the enterprises started by this powerful man. He improved the course of the Conwy itself in order to bring boats up to Gwydir, and actively encouraged local industries such as weaving and fishing. But in the end tradition is unforgiving, and his soul is said to be condemned to remain, trapped for ever, under the Swallow Falls waterfall at Betws-y-coed.

*Ffridd Uchaf ('the highest pasture') in the shadow of Snowdon
insert: Hafod y Llan, Beddgelert*

Hafod and Hendre

The history of land-use in the valleys around Eryri is a matter of the development of natural resources, and the most important of these was of course the land itself. Forest clearance probably started to make an impact on the valley slopes in the fifth or sixth centuries. From the occupation of cleared land in the form of round-hut settlements and associated field systems, there developed the medieval farmsteads centred on the long hut, a transition from the ancient hut circle to the modern farmhouse. These, where it has been possible to date them, seem to belong to the 14th and 15th centuries.

It was from those in turn that the upland farm developed, and during the succeeding centuries right up to our own an effective system of co-operation between the hills and the valley arose, the double use of the ''hafod' and the 'hendre'. This involved a system known to geography as seasonal transhumance, the movement of stock from valley to hill land in the spring, and back to the valley for the winter. It is a practice which still in effect continues today, but in the age of landrovers and tractors it is possible to work the two farms from the greater comfort of the valley. The crucial difference is that previously the whole family went too, and the result must have been a shift of population counterparting the great movement of flocks which we can still see taking place.

The hafod, the '*summer dwelling*', was the seasonally-inhabited upland farm which no longer exists. Many of them stand in ruins on the tracks up to the lakes and high 'cwms' of Eryri – Cowlyd, Eigiau, Nant Peris and Nant Gwynant. Although the habit of wholesale transhumance declined during the last century, and it is probably more than a hundred years now since any family made the seasonal movement to the hafod in the spring and back to the hendre, '*the old homestead*', for the harvest, several of the old hafod farms remained in occupation by sheepfarmers within living memory.

The fact that it has been actively and continuously farmed is largely responsible for the present appearance of the landscape. The valleys a maze of hedged fields, the upland slopes kept bare of scrub by the persistent browsing of sheep; and everywhere that feature so characteristic of Welsh landscape, the great dry-stone walls, stretching across the mountains for mile after mile.

Hendre Wen, on the floor of the Conwy valley

High field patterns on Tal y Fan above the Conwy valley

Stone wall and ffriddoedd

These strongly-built structures arose during the last century in connection both with the seasonal use of valley and hill, and with the mixed farming of both sheep and cattle. The 'mountain wall' along the contour limits the height below which the sheep are brought in the winter and the cattle permanently contained. The walls climbing the ridges, on the other hand, are mainly the boundaries of property. They are not essentially intended to prevent the straying of flocks, since the mountain sheep are quite capable of scaling them, and since this is anyway effected by another means. The sheep of this area have an inbred tendency to remain on the 'cynefin', the pasture which goes with the farm and on which they were reared. This conditioning is passed

Trefriw Woollen Mill and traditional Welsh tweed

67

*Tŷ Mawr Wybrnant, the birthplace of Bishop William Morgan,
the translator of the Bible into Welsh*

from ewe to lamb generation after generation, and it means that if a mountain farm changes hands the flock must pass with it.

Not only the farming traditions but the stock itself are part of a very old-established system. The original local breeds of both sheep and cattle still predominate in the valley's farms. They are hardy and economic, and permit the efficient use of otherwise marginal land. The Welsh Black cattle, probably among Britain's oldest breeds, are fine sturdy animals, with long curved horns. The Welsh mountain sheep as exemplified here are also probably an original British breed, ideally adapted to this terrain. They are small but compact and well-fleshed, agile and sure-footed, with exceptionally thick fleeces. The rams are decorated with magnificent curved horns.

That, the farming of cattle and mountain sheep, is the valley's oldest and most enduring industry. It gave rise to several effects at an early date which continue to influence the valley life. The development of Llanrwst into the substantial agricultural centre which it now is, and has been for generations, was perhaps one of the most prominent of these. At first a point of travel, it is now essentially the valley's market town. Of great importance to the other valley settlements also was the use of one of the area's products, the treating and working of wool.

From the beginning, wool had been turned into cloth on the spot, rather than exported in its raw form. Until the start of the last century this was largely a cottage industry, but from the early 1800's the idea of centralising the process at a village mill began to take root in North Wales. In our area, a water-powered woollen-mill occurred first at Penmachno, in the second decade of the 19th century, where the mill still forms a prominent part of the village. And in the heart of the valley at Trefriw the business of cloth weaving became a major industry, and has remained so to the present day. The fine, substantial woollen-mill there now is a successor to generations of mills at Trefriw, which was evidently a milling centre even before it became a cloth-weaving one, as far back as the 14th century. The typical Welsh weave produced there from the fleeces of local mountain sheep is superior in quality to its early predecessors, but retains the warmth and durability to which they owed their success. Another working mill can be seen at Bryncir, at the head of Cwm Pennant valley, one of the western valleys of Eryri.

The use of water-power enabled this product of agricultural enterprises to become an industry. It was, of course, not an invention for this purpose but

Llanrwst bridge – an important crossing by an old ford and the factor in the development of Llanrwst as a market town for eastern Eryri

Tu hwnt i'r bont, Llanrwst

an imitation of something already taking place, since corn had been ground by water-power for centuries. An old corn-mill with its wheel still in place may be seen on the upper Conwy at Ysbyty Ifan, and in this case the old use of water-power was adapted to modern times by the fitting of a turbine in the 1930's, by means of which it supplied the whole village with electricity until the early 1960's.

As well as having a rich heritage of farming and droving history, the high valleys of Eryri have their place in Welsh culture as the nurture of poets and writers. Between the Lledr and the Machno valleys, is a special place of pilgrimage. Tŷ Mawr Wybrnant is a solidly built old house set in its own valley in the hills, lovingly restored and maintained by the National Trust. Its eminent importance in Welsh culture is due to the fact that it was the birthplace, in 1545, of William Morgan, who became Bishop of St Asaph at the time when Sir John Wynn, was presiding over his great estates at Gwydir, in the Conwy valley. Bishop Morgan has the distinction of being the first translator of the complete Bible into Welsh, and Tŷ Mawr now houses a fine collection of early Welsh Bibles in memory of this.

Loading slate on boats on Llyn Peris

Porthmadog slate quay

Slate and Railway

Slate has been used as a building material at least from Roman times. It was in use in the Middle Ages and roofs began to be commonly made of it during the sixteenth century. Of course it was more commonly used, both by the Romans and the Norman castle-builders, in areas where it was plentifully available. We hear of it early in North Wales. As early as the fourteenth century slate was exported from here to roof Chester castle. In the time of Elizabeth I there was a healthy export trade to Ireland, single slates selling at 1/8d per thousand, doubles at 2/8d. Some three to four hundred thousand slates were sold to Ireland in the ten years after 1583.

The word comes from the Old French 'escalate', as also does the English word 'slat', meaning a splinter, something fractured or split. As was explained in an earlier chapter it gets its fissile property from the parallel arrangement of its particules, itself the result of the mode of its formation, by extreme pressure from one direction. Its abundance in the area of the lower Ogwen and Peris valleys has had a profound effect on the region.

The trade with Ireland which started so early became, in the eighteenth century, then underpinning of the future industry. From about 1721 trade to the continent of Europe reinforced this. In the 1730's Caernarfon was exporting around two million slates a year.

This was not then an organised business. From the early 1700's the Vaynol estate, which owned the area of the parishes of Llanberis and Llanddeiniolen, in which the most accessible slate lay, had absent owners. Sporadic private quarrying at this time allowed a large number of individual shallow quarries to develop on the east bank of Llyn Peris. Increasing demand towards the middle of the century led to the merging of these into partnerships. By 1772 there were five such partnerships in operation above Padarn and Peris.

Penrhyn at that time also had an absent owner. The Williams family had remained in occupation until 1684, but in the early eighteenth century the estate became split between two co-heirs, one of whom lived in Devon and London, the other in Cheshire. In 1765, however, the Williams heiress married John Pennant, a rich sugar planter returned from the West Indies, a man from the same ancient Flintshire family as the writer and traveller Thomas Pennant. He at once started to buy out his wife's co-owner's interest in the Penrhyn estate, and then to let off leases to quarry in the area around

Slate fence and Penrhyn quarry

Bethesda memorial to quarry strikers

Dinworwig's quarry terraces above Llyn Peris

what is now Bethesda. This set a pattern which was to be repeated for the rest of that century: Penrhyn and Vaynol alternated in innovation, but each carefully watched the other's moves.

When Thomas Pennant made his journey through North Wales in 1773 the slate industry was already a prominent part of the economy. 'The quarries are becoming now the source of a prodigious commerce,' he says, annually exporting 'many millions of slaters.' Lord Penrhyn 'has added greatly to the population of the country by the improvements he has made in the slate business.' The passage, however, owes not a little to hindsight, and must have been a revision from a later phase of his tours, since John Pennant was succeeded by his son Richard in 1781, and the latter did not become the first Baron Penrhyn (an Irish peerage) until 1783.

It is true that it was due to him that the slate business flourished. Unlike his father, who simply let the quarries, he took the whole lot in hand, systematically buying out the leases and not renewing them as they expired, until he could manage the business as a single unit. This was the start of the Penrhyn quarries at Bethesda. From about 1780 onwards the effects of the Industrial Revolution on the construction industry accelerated, as the introduction of steam power led to a concentration of the workforce around purpose-built factories, and hence the building of many uniform terraced dwellings. For these (and indeed the factories themselves) a seemingly insatiable demand for standard-sized roofing slates had come about.

Vaynol, meanwhile, the estate which owned the other side of the Elidyr mountains and hence the western end of that mass of slate, had been taken over in 1787 by a consortium of businessmen, who rented the quarrying areas on a twenty-one year lease from its absent owner and thus founded the Dinorwic Slate Company. By 1791 this was exporting from Caernarfon some two and a half million slates a year.

Vaynol, in fact, controlled Caernarfon as a port, obliging the Penrhyn slates to leave from the river mouth known as Aber Cegin, where, in 1790, Lord Penrhyn built a port. Pennant tells us that in 1792 'upwards of twelve thousand tons were exported' from there. Porth Penrhyn was a busy place, always thronged with vessels. From there, says Pennant, 'the slates are sent to Liverpool, and up the Mersey by means of the canal to all the internal parts of the kingdom, and to Hull; from whence is a second exportation: numbers are shipped for Ireland, for Flanders, and even the West Indies.' He also

Dorothea, Nantlle valley   *Llechwedd's underground car*

*An underground party visiting the slate caverns of Llechwedd,
Blaenau Ffestiniog*

mentions that the production of writing slates was a Penrhyn speciality.

Transport, of course, was always a problem to the slate industry. A tramway ran from Penrhyn quarries to Porth Penrhyn from 1801. In this Vaynol lagged a little behind. It was not until 1824 that a tramway connected the Dinorwig quarries with the then new port of Port Dinorwig.

The outbreak of war with France in 1793 put a sharp break on the construction business and halved the exports from Port Penrhyn. A war tax on slates of 20 per cent and upwards penalised the coastal trade. Business recovered with the Peace of Amiens in 1801, and a few years later the Battle of Trafalgar made the seas safer for shipping. By 1809 Port Penrhyn was shipping slates to Boston, Massachusetts.

All this of course had an immense effect on this remote and unpropitious area. In the first forty years of the last century the populations of the quarrying areas doubled and in some areas trebled. New towns came into existence around the slate terraces. In 1820 a group of Non-Conformists, themselves mainly quarrymen, built themselves a chapel near their new working quarters and called it, after the biblical pool with healing waters, Bethesda. The rise of Welsh Non-Conformism at this time gives a strangely biblical look to the map of North Wales, since the habit was to name the new Independent chapels after Old or New Testament places or characters: Ebenezer, Carmel, Bethel, Saron, Nebo. Pubs, cottages and more chapels quickly followed these remote foundations. By 1865, with a population of five to six thousand, Bethesda was four times that of the whole of its parish in 1801.

Another feature which was partly spurred by the expansion of the industry was the improvement of the roads. When Pennant first visited Nant Ffrancon he descended into it by 'a most dreadful horse path . . . worked in the rudest manner into steps'. Some twenty years later he reports that 'a noble coach road is made, even beyond Nant Ffrancon'. This was Lord Penrhyn's work, and it set the future pattern of communications. When Telford was commissioned, in 1817, to route the London to Ireland road through North Wales, he used Lord Penrhyn's stretch of coach road, and hence the new main road ran, conveniently, right past Penrhyn quarries. Road building, at that time, was seen partly as a form of poor relief, since the ending of the war had led to a slump and widespread poverty.

As both construction and industry picked up again after the war the slate

The Welsh National Slate Museum at Llanberis

Slate slabs at the museum

*The old craft of splitting slate
displayed at the museum*

business boomed again, profits of around £7,000 in 1820 increasing to £30,000 in the 1850's and more than £90,000 by 1861. All was not however by any means harmonious. Right from the start the industry had been run on a system of bargaining between quarrymen and owners, and given the hard conditions and the power possessed by the workforce in a demand-led market it was not long before industrial unrest became systematic. A strike at Penrhyn in 1825 shocked the whole industry, and was settled with the remedy of some grievances. By 1874 the workers were better organised, and able to deal with the owners on more equal terms. This however was not a situation which the Penrhyn family intended to continue. A lock-out in 1896 was evidently effective, since this response was tried again in 1900. The famous three year lock-out which then followed probably had a decisive effect on the future of the slate industry as a whole. Although of course it enabled the Dinorwig quarries to boom, without Penrhyn in operation the national supply of slates was unable to meet demand, with the result of the commodity becoming overpriced in relation to competing materials. With a change in tastes and house-styles in the new century slate roofs were seen, in the new suburbias, as urban and old-fashioned. so that those who could have afforded what had now become something of a luxury no longer wanted it, and in spite of a revival in the late 1940's to serve the post-war rebuilding programme the industry never again reached the heights it had achieved in the mid-nineteenth century.

When the Dinorwig Quarry closed in 1969 its substantial repair and maintenance workshops were abandoned but left standing. Being so solidly built they have remained much as they were, and now house 'The Welsh National Slate Museum', a working museum, part of the Padarn Country Park. This complex in general forms a tourist facility of the highest quality, and gives a useful insight into the industrial history of the mountains. Indeed with the pumped-storage power station almost alongside, occupying the base of the closed quarries, it is clear that the industrial use of Snowdonia's natural assets still goes on.

The National Slate Museum still has much working machinery, and displays the quality and surprising versatility of slate. It is worth a visit if only to experience a sense of the astonishing power of its gigantic water wheel. This giant, the largest in mainland Britain, was erected in 1870, worked until 1925, and is now restored to running order. Fifty feet in

*Penrhyn castle, the home of the
Penrhyn quarry owners*

Plas Tan y Bwlch

Vaynol Hall, near Bangor

diameter, it produces eighty horse-power and runs all the wheels and cogs of the foundry and all the workshops, this free power for ever being created simply by the weight of the water which falls gently into the giant wheel's buckets. It rumbles with the hum of serious business, the implication of power. In a world in which much is often fake it shocks you to come up against something so real. This is serious. This is no toy.

The quarries at Blaenau Ffestiniog were in operation before the end of the 18th century, but it took the entrepreneurial and administrative skills of one forceful man, the young (as he was then) Samuel Holland, who arrived in 1821 to sort out his father's business, to spot and seize the providential opportunity. In just four years he had built there a major business.

Progress feeds on itself. Holland could not have got his quarry's 10,000 tons a year of slates out from Blaenau and around the world if he had continued the age-old means of transport. On the backs of pack animals to the valley floor, then in carts down to the Dwyryd, by small boat down the shallow river to load the beached schooners on the tidal sandbanks, the slates made their painstaking progress. Holland changed all that.

Railways were not new, when Samuel Holland, having acquired a quay in the new harbour of Porthmadog, succeeded in getting a railway bill through Parliament, against local opposition, in 1833. Quarries had used wagonways since the sixteenth century. They were not even new in North Wales, since Lord Penrhyn had a five mile track built between 1800 and 1801 to connect his quarry to the port called by the same name, Port Penrhyn. A railway ran from Caernarfon to the slate quarries at Nantlle from 1824-5, which also took copper ore from Drws-y-coed. What was new about this particular railway was that, right from the start, it carried passengers.

These early railways were powered by horses and by gravity, and Holland's, to start with, was no exception. 'All went up,' he himself wrote, 'to the inclines in carriages drawn by horses, but we all came down without horses, the inclination being sufficient to enable us to do so.' The horses came down in the train as well, 'feeding all the way'.

That was in 1838, and it made the Ffestiniog railway the first public light railway in the world. It is notable too for its narrow gauge, which Holland was advised would be cheaper to construct and 'less to pay for the land taken'. This characteristic proved influential, and experiments here in the 1860's led

The Welsh Highland Railway at Porthmadog

Tan y Bwlch station on Ffestiniog Railway

to the adoption of a similar form in light railways elsewhere in Britain and in North America.

In the meantime another innovation was taking place. Steam power replaced horses in many places from the 1830's, and in 1863 it reached the Ffestiniog valley. At first it was thought that the narrow track and the sharp curves would make this impossible, but Holland had a nephew as enterprising as himself who drew up his own design.

Remarkably this pioneering line is still in operation, in fact forming one of North Wales major visitor attractions. In 1996 it carried 327,000 people. Its industrial purpose has of course given way to the exploitation of North Wales' major asset, its unrivalled scenery. Now conveniently joining up at Blaenau Ffestiniog with the branch line up the Conwy valley (itself started in the 1860's) it offers a railway experience which it would be hard to match.

It was in fact partly the further development of the Conwy valley line in the 1870's that led to the decline of the Ffestiniog line. Another railway also reached Blaenau Ffestiniog from Bala, and down in the valley of the Dwyryd the use of the port of Porthmadog was itself challenged by the construction of the Cambrian Coast Line, which could take slates from Minffordd southwards to link up with the growing network. Patterns of communication were changing, and so, during the first decades of this century, were types of roofing material. By the 1920's the Ffestiniog narrow-gauge was largely a tourist attraction, and during the war it closed to passengers. In August 1946 it closed completely, and lay abandoned. Work started on restoration in 1954 and by 1982 the complete line was rehabilitated. It remains largely staffed by volunteers.

If the Ffestiniog narrow-gauge has changed its nature, from conveying 130,000 tons of slate a year at its peak to its current score of 327,000 passengers, Porthmadog's other light railway was designed to carry tourists from the start. The Welsh Highland Railway, built in the 1920's was in effect a link between the Ffestiniog narrow-gauge and yet another stretch of line, formerly called the North Wales Narrow Gauge Railway, which crossed to the coast south of Caernarfon. This was never the success it was expected to be, and in due course it closed and became a footpath until the renewed interest in light railways led to the formation of a company to reopen it, at the end of the 1990's.

Railways are not the only legacy left to tourism by slate. Blaenau

Ffestiniog now has a declining population and lack of industrial base, but it boasts two major tourist attractions, the Llechwedd slate caverns and the Gloddfa Ganol slate mine and quarry. These provide views of the old workings and an insight into the history of the industry.

In 2010, the final link of the narrow-gauge Welsh Highland Railway, connecting slate quarries with the ports of Caernarfon and Porthmadog, was re-opened as a tourist attraction. Narrow-gauge railways now connect Caernarfon with Porthmadog and Porthmadog with Blaenau Ffestiniog, offering access to a wide choice of walking routes and other attractions from the various stations en route.

One other legacy of the quarrying of the mountains is the great estates of the quarry-owners with their country houses. Even the lesser quarries, such as the one called after its owners, the Oakley family, north of Maentwrog, which survived in use until 1971, produced the fine seat, Plas Tan y Bwlch, which is now a study centre run by the National Park Authority. At Vaynol, on the Menai Strait, the Assheton-Smith family, when they eventually came back to North Wales to run their quarries, built alongside the original Elizabethan mansion a fine country house which perhaps incorporates a smaller early eighteenth century one. There is no doubt that one of the most striking and historically complex developments arising out of the value of slate was the succession of events at Penrhyn.

The descendants of Ednyfed Fychan, the lieutenant of Llywelyn the Great, possessed a large amount of land in the later middle ages, and one of the most notable of them, Gwilym ap Gruffudd, built himself a house at Penrhyn in the early fifteenth century. He expanded his lands by purchase until the estate covered almost the whole of the parish of Llandegai. The family took the surname Griffith, when Henry VIII recommended that the Welsh gentry adopt hereditary names and the Acts of incorporation of England and Wales encouraged this. Gwilym's descendants also owned the Cochwillan estate (where the house, a fifteenth century hall, has been recently restored to habitable use), and confusingly adapted the first of his names rather than the second and called themselves Williams.

Griffiths resided at Penrhyn until the sixteenth century, when it was bought by their cousin John Williams of Cochwillan. Williams was an ecclesiastic who was already, and was to become more so, prominent in British politics. He was made Lord Keeper of the Privy Seal in 1621, and bought Penrhyn in 1622. He went on to become Archbishop of York, and played a significant part in the Civil War.

The estate, as we have seen earlier in this chapter, became eventually split, and was restored to unity by the Pennant family, who both bought and married into it. Richard Pennant in 1785 bought out the remaining shares. When in 1808 he died childless his widow remained there for some years, but the property had been left to a cousin, George Dawkins, who, between 1821 and 1835, built the castle.

If this grotesque monument to pretension seems laughable to us now, we have to remember the late 18th century taste for the Gothic and the Picturesque. It was not until just after the Napoleonic wars that circumstances combined to enable the building of follies on a truly vast scale. The ending of the war left the country poor, unemployment out of control and starvation a constant threat for many. At the same time it revitalised the construction industry, and hence the market for slate and stone.

It remains a choice as to whether one describes the building of these massive structures, and the great walls around the parks of estates such as this and that of Vaynol, as a form of 'poor relief'; or as the exploitation of fortuitously cheap labour. The two are different facets of the same thing, the choice of phrase a statement of one's point of view rather than historical fact. Gwrych Castle near Abergele is a good example of this scale of landscape decoration by a quarry-owner, and being finished in about 1816 it may well have influenced Dawkins. He commissioned the architect Thomas Hopper, who had done some work for the Prince of Wales, to design and supervise the work.

The Pennant family lived in Penrhyn for at least some of the time from its completion until 1949. (Dawkins had taken the name on his inheritance, which now, by subsequent marriage, has become Douglas-Pennant). In 1951 the Castle, together with a large area of upland farms, was donated in lieu of death duties to the Inland Revenue, and the whole of this handed over to the National Trust. The Castle, which had been open to the public sporadically from the start, is now a popular tourist attraction.

The ascent to the summit of Snowdon

Early travellers in Eryri

Men and Mountains

Lord Lyttleton, in the middle of the eighteenth century, referred to them as 'the formidable mountains of Snowdon'. He saw them as 'black and naked rocks, which seem to be piled one above the other; the summits of some of them are covered with clouds, and cannot be ascended'.

To all the early travellers Snowdon was a fearful place, and best avoided. Giraldus, in the twelfth century, had been awed by the sight of the mountains from Anglesey; Leland in the sixteenth said they were 'Horrible with the sighte of bare stones'. Camden, his contemporary, called them the British Alps, and said they were snow-covered all year round. The first people actually to approach them, apart from local shepherds, were intrepid botanists, such as the Reverend Bingley, who, in pursuit of rare plants, actually climbed Clogwyn Du'r Arddu, in 1798. It is perhaps Thomas Pennant, who may be called the first tourist, who first paid attention to the mountains for their own sake, climbing Snowdon by the miners' track. It was largely Wordsworth who brought the romantic view of nature and Britain's wilder places to the popular imagination. Writing about the turn of the century he set the last part of 'The Prelude' on Snowdon itself, where he describes a summer night-time climb to see the dawn. The grandeur of the mountain in the moonlight moved him to thoughts of God and infinity. The romantic age had arrived.

Once the fashion started artists and romantic writers flocked to the mountains. We shall see in the next chapter how the formation of an artists' colony is at the basis of the history of Betws-y-coed. The penetration of observers into the heart of the mountains was accelerated, from the early years of the century, by Lord Penrhyn's new turnpike. This ran from Capel Curig to the coast from 1802, and Lord Penrhyn added an inn to it, now Plas y Brenin, to which the various travellers came. A further road ran down the Llanberis Pass from 1830, and connected the Capel Curig turnpike with Beddgelert, where there were further hostelries, already, now the Saracen's Head and the Goat.

We get our clearest insight into the mountain area of the nineteenth century from George Borrow, who came up the Capel Curig road on foot in the 1850's. He dined at the Royal Hotel, as it became, where he felt conspicuous in his walking clothes 'amidst a great deal of fashionable

Llanberis: The Victoria Hotel

Penygwryd Hotel

company'. When he later climbed Snowdon he was not alone either: 'We were far from being the only visitors to the hill this day; groups of people, or single individuals, might be seen going up or descending the path as far as the eye could reach'. This familiar scene to us now was even then not new. In 1831 a visitor had recorded: 'There is no place more public than the higher ground of Eryri during the summer'. It was remarked in 1857 that 'Snowdon is ascended by everyone because it is the highest top . . . ' The path, Borrow remarks, was surprisingly good. The place had, it is clear, already begun to turn into a country park. A photograph of the summit in the 1870's shows a shanty town of shacks crowded with people and horses.

Some time around the middle of that century attention began to shift from the achievement of reaching the summit to the challenge of doing so by harder means. The walker came up the prepared track from Llanberis. The mountaineer saw Snowdon from its sharper side.

Already by the 1840's the farmhouse at Penygwryd had begun to double as an inn. In 1847 it was bought by a young farmer, Harry Owen, who ran it as a hostelry with his wife for the next forty-four years. Charles Kingsley depicts it in his novel 'Two Years Ago' published in 1857. Going in, you found 'a low room ceiled with dark beams, from which hung bacon and fishing-rods, harness and drying stockings, and all the miscellanea of a fishing inn kept by a farmer, and beneath it the usual happy, hearty, honest group'. Such was the success of this that in 1859 the inn was largely reconstructed. Kingsley himself came mainly for the fishing, but the inn was at the time frequented by famous Alpine climbers. The Climbers Club was in due course founded there, towards the turn of the century. But by then Mr and Mrs Owen had died, and with their going a change of fashion took place. The state of Penygwryd having deteriorated, its place in the climbing world was usurped by the inn founded by the 'younger' or 'new' Owens at Pen-y-pass. This became the centre of activity from 1900.

It was a literary and academic crowd, and in those years before the Great War seems to have had its own inbuilt nostalgia. It was a hearty and healthy scene, ' . . . with Frank Smythe, perhaps, crooning on his mouth-organ, perched in a bath towel on the back of the bench; Tony Smyth, the notable airman, and Humphrey Trevelyan, now the Ambassador to Egypt, or O'Brien and Longland, in abstract argument, through the steam; and George Mallory or young George Trevelyan leaping to do slow circles over the roof-beam . . . '

An early mountain and botanical guide

So Geoffrey Winthrop Young recalls, with unmistakable regret, the lost innocence of those days at Pen-y-pass 'before the war'.

The Great War changed the face of climbing as it changed so much else. Winthrop Young, writing (as above) in 'Snowdon Biography', in the 1950's, puts it thus: 'The war came; and it eliminated much of the more leisured class, and destroyed the balance between work and cultivated leisure'. It was, in fact, partly a social change. But with the sudden increase in accessibility which came with common car ownership in the 20's and 30's came also a change in attitude to the mountains. It was now no longer a question of coming in a group for some weeks during university vacations. Snowdon could be reached at the weekend from the midlands or Merseyside. This affected (as Winthrop Young puts it) 'the social elements from which climbers were drawn'. It also meant something more serious for the future of the sport. The focus before the war had always been on climbing mountains. Now it became (with more frequent attempts now possible on the same routes) a matter of climbing rocks.

Cliffs, such as Clogwyn Du'r Arddu or Lliwedd, had been used as practice grounds for some time, but always on the understanding that the techniques learnt were for the purpose of ascending peaks. Suddenly in the 1920's that outlook changed. Geoffrey Sutton, writing in the same invaluable book, identifies the moment as 'Fred Pigott's ascent of the East Buttress of Clogwyn Du'r Arddu in 1927'. Certainly the names of Pigott, Frank Smythe and Morley Wood are essential to the annals of the origins of rock-climbing. With the change in emphasis, and the change in the social class of those now enjoying the mountains, came a shift away from the hotels, as Young again says, 'in their happy solitude at the remote end of long walks and slow cart-drives' towards 'the coming of the hostel, the climbing hut, and the camp'. With this change in the 1920's yet another could be seen to be on the way.

When the focus moved from the mountain to the rock it soon led to attention to technique; and this in turn raised the question of the permissible limit of aids such as tools and mechanisms. When Morley Wood carried some stones up the Clogwyn in his pocket to jam into cracks, he opened up a vast debate. It was decided at the time that a stone native to the cliff might be restored, but not a foreign one introduced. Young comments: ' . . . we may now see the jammed stone as the thin end of a prodigious wedge, embodying an alteration not natural to the mountain and predicating immediately the metal peg, the hammer, and the pulley'.

Thus yet again a new era of climbing is born, and after the second world war it boomed again. Rock-climbers, like everyone else, seem to grow younger. Colin Kirkus was nineteen when he developed new routes on the Clogwyn and on Tryfan; Joe Brown was twenty when he revolutionised the routes on the Clogwyn in the summer of 1951. By then Chris Briggs was at the Penygwryd, where in the early 50's the British Everest team were to make their base for training, and a new awareness of the mountains arose among the writers and broadcasters who might be found there.

All this is satisfactorily recorded in 'Snowdon Biography', itself a sequel, as it makes clear, to Carr and Lister's magisterial 'The Mountains of Snowdonia'. For a personal insight into what it was actually like to live there nothing could improve on Thomas Firbank's 'I Bought a Mountain', recently re-issued, in which by a magical facility of style Firbank evokes the hill country in all its moods.

Waterloo bridge on the A5 at Betws-y-coed

Thomas Telford

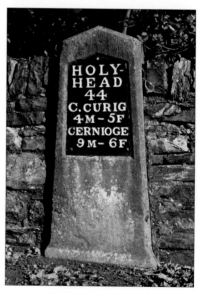

A Telford milestone at Betws-y-coed

The Advent of Tourism

We saw in the last chapter that when people started to come to visit North Wales they did so, at first, for a particular purpose; as botanists, for the purpose of scientific research; as mountaineers, later as rock-climbers. The high rainfall of the area gives the plentiful run-off required to form trout streams, and people came as anglers too, fishing its streams, rivers and lakes. Those who were also writers spread news of the area's beauty, which gradually enticed others to come just to view its landscape. It was only really when fashionable society could see this landscape itself, for instance hanging on the walls of the Royal Academy in London, that the habit developed of making the journey just for the sake of being there.

Improved roads facilitated this. For a long time the network of narrow drover's roads, which connected the areas of upland pasture to the market towns, and the long-neglected Roman roads were all we had, and this combination kept the area isolated. In the eighteenth century through routes became developed with the formation of turnpike trusts (by which a commercial body was granted a lease, usually of twenty-one years, on a stretch of road, empowered to levy tolls in recompense for maintaining the carriageway). It was perhaps the formation of the Capel Curig Turnpike Trust in 1802 which started the trend to increasing accessibility which still continues. This linked to Lord Penrhyn's road from the coast to Capel Curig, and for the first time provided a serviceable through route through the mountains. The Royal Hotel, built as a coaching inn on this route, has now, as Plas y Brenin, become a major outdoor pursuit centre.

By 1808 the Shrewsbury to Holyhead mail-coach was using this. The importance of the route through Wales had increased greatly with the Act of Union with Ireland, which came into effect in 1801, and by the second decade of that century the turnpike system was beginning to look inadequate. Thomas Telford was commissioned to survey the roads through North Wales in 1811, and between 1815 and 1819 he rebuilt the road which is now the A5, in the process absorbing into his new route the Capel Curig turnpike. This involved the building of the Waterloo Bridge at Betws, which was opened in 1816.

Meanwhile the artists had begun to make North Wales' scenery famous. The distinguished art historian Peter Lord has written the definitive history

Swallow Falls, near Betws-y-coed

The Royal Oak hotel, Betws-y-coed

of 'The Betws-y-coed Artists' Colony' (published by the National Library of Wales), from which it is clear that the movement largely stems from the enthusiasm for the area of the highly regarded Royal Academician David Cox. Cox was a watercolour painter, who used the medium to convey an immediate response to what he saw before him, as he painted, in all weathers, in the open air.

Lord makes it clear that although Cox was not the first artist to paint in the Betws area, the fact that he made his base there drew others to do likewise. Before that artists had painted the area while passing through it. In the 1770's Moses Griffiths had depicted the area as the illustrator of Pennant's 'Tours'. Also in the 1770's Paul Sandby was one of the first to depict, in watercolour, the North Wales mountain scenery. Turner came in 1798, again travelling through; he came again in 1802, on which occasion he painted his famous view of Dolbadarn Castle. Cox himself had visited in 1805 and 6, and in 1836 contributed to make that inn his base when he came to stay in 1844, then aged sixty-one, and every year from then.

The Royal Oak thus became the centre of the artists' colony, which rapidly grew around Cox. It was a much simpler building then, having been several times rebuilt, 'a short, dark passage' (writes the contemporary William Hall) leading to 'the parlour, reserved for the company of "the higher order" . . . Bacon and hams hung from the kitchen ceiling . . . '

Betws was a quiet place when Cox discovered it, two or three inns and one small shop, beautifully depicted in Thomas Creswick's engraving of 1836. A few years after had made it his base it was described as overflowing with artists. You met them round every bend, on their way to or from their sketching grounds, their white tents and umbrellas 'to be seen in whichever direction the eye turned, suggested to the visitor the encampment of an invading army'. So again remarks Hall.

It is clear from their work that the artists were attracted by exactly the same things as are the tourists today. They painted Pont y Pair, the seventeenth century bridge which carried the old Llanrwst road across the river Llugwy. They painted the Swallow Falls, of course. They went up to Capel Curig to paint the three peaks of Snowdon.

Travel for its own sake, and for the enjoyment of the scenery, was largely a 19th century innovation, pioneered as far as Snowdonia is concerned by writers such as Pennant and George Borrow. From the start the valleys were

The Goat Hotel, Beddgelert

The Snowdon Railway station at Llanberis

ready to provide facilities, and the spa at Trefriw (its waters still flowing, though at present little used) was a flourishing and fashionable centre of relaxation when watering-places were in vogue.

Travel, moreover, was boosted and facilitated by a new means of transport at this time. During the 1860's the branch line from Llandudno Junction was developed, completed to Betws-y-coed by 1868. It still provides by far the best way of viewing the valley's scenery, a journey of great variety and spectacular effect which can stand comparison with the world's more famous rail trips. By this means visitors may now travel through the mountains to Blaenau Ffestiniog, where the Ffestiniog narrow-gauge railway joins up with this line from its long climb up from the other coast, and where too the two slate-quarrying museums of Llechwedd and Gloddfa Ganol offer a fascinating insight into the workings of some of the largest slate-producing undertakings in the world.

Down in the Conwy valley another of our present major attractions came into being in the 19th century. In 1875 Mr Henry Pochin chose a valley near Eglwysbach in which to found his ideal garden, and Bodnant Gardens now

Bodnant Gardens

97

Hafod Eryri at the summit of Snowdon

display in their full maturity the realisation of his plans. The soil and climate of this secluded spot favour the spring shrubs for which the gardens are rightly famous, and they are best seen as early as possible in the open season. The home farm on the main road has now been converted to house a centre for the promotion of local produce.

Portmeirion, like so much we have considered in this area, is the result of the determination and creativity of a single forceful individual. The late Sir Clough Williams-Ellis acquired an overgrown headland and started to clear its undergrowth in 1926, having identified its mild climate and secluded position as being the perfect situation for his romantic vision

Portmeirion

Beddgelert – a popular centre for walkers

Outdoor activities at Plas y Brenin, Capel Curig

of an ideal village. The land had previously belonged to his uncle, once the site of a small settlement and landscaped with tree-planting and rhododendrons during the mid-19th century.

Sir Clough (who died in 1978 at the age of 94) was a largely self-trained architect, the descendant of Caernarfonshire landowners, who became fashionable and successful in London in the 1920's. His work may be seen in various parts of the country and the world, but particularly in his home area, where his liking for urns and pedestals has left his distinctive mark on the gateways and grounds of many country houses. He it was who designed the grave of Lloyd George at Llanystumdwy, bringing together two of the powerful personalities of this area. A man very much in the mould of Madocks, he is rightly described in *The Times*'s obituary as 'his own best work'.

Having first converted the old house by the sea to a hotel, Williams-Ellis began to collect from various parts of the country interesting and rare buildings, which he had dismantled, transported and re-erected at Portmeirion. The result is a fanciful and amusing world, a total environment intended only to please.

Tourism approached as well from the other direction, and early in the century the old inns of Beddgelert were becoming substantial hotels. With the opening of the Snowdon Mountain Railway in 1896 the sanctuary of the numinous mountain was finally breached. The old and unsatisfactory 'hotel' on the summit has now been magnificently replaced by the 'Hafod Eryri' facility, a massive undertaking costing more than £8 million, opened in June 2009. We have to be thankful that it is only in the summer that the summit becomes so congested with people who quite clearly could not have walked there.

Very many people, however, do; and this causes an increasing problem. Snowdon suffers worst, of course, because Snowdon is and always has been where everybody wants to be. The erosion of the paths by the sheer number of boots has led to a wholesale paving programme which has reduced much of the mountain to the character of a municipal park. The alternative, which no-one would recommend, is to be seen now even on the less popular peaks; the white scar of ever-widening track, as water erodes the top soil of trodden turf and walkers use the sides of the slippery shaly wound and so

Castell y Gwynt at sunrise

inadvertently make it larger. Since limiting visitor numbers would seem distasteful also there appears to be no solution apart from continuous, and one hopes sensitive, cosmetic treatment.

Cars too harm the scenery by their sheer numbers during the summer months. No-one knows exactly how many people come to Eryri, but a survey done in 1994 by the National Park Authority estimated that it had 6.6 million visitor days devoted to it per year. This represents undoubtedly a lot of people. Those not constrained by the bounds of school holidays can still catch the magic of which Wordsworth said

> . . . it appeared to me the type
> Of a majestic intellect, its acts
> And its possession, what it has and craves,
> What in itself it is, and would become.
> There I beheld the emblem of a mind
> That feeds upon infinity, that broods
> Over the dark abyss.

Other history and heritage titles
by Michael Senior

Visit: www.carreg-gwalch.com